The Kingd

by Michael Ryall

Table of Contents

Introduction

Nubia was a **region** in Africa. Nubia had a **kingdom** before **Kush**. Then Nubia had the kingdom of Kush.

Read to learn about the first kingdom. Learn about the kingdom of Kush. Learn why Kush was important.

Words to Know

 Egypt

 Kerma

 kingdom

 Kush

 Meroe

 Napata

 Nile River

 Nubia

 region

See the Glossary on page 22. 3

What Was Nubia?

Nubia was a region in Africa. The **Nile River** was in Nubia. The Nile River had waterfalls.

▲ Nubia was in Africa.

▲ The Nile had waterfalls.

THEN AND NOW

The region was named Nubia long ago. Now the region is part of Sudan. Sudan is a country in Africa.

Some people traveled on the Nile River. Some people traded goods.

People traded gold. ▶

Other people were farmers. They used Nile River water for crops.

▲ **People farmed beside the Nile River.**

Nubia had a kingdom. The kingdom was **Kerma**. Kerma was a city. Kerma had land around it.

1st Cataract

EGYPT

RED SE

NILE RIVER

2nd Cataract

IT'S A FACT

The people of Kerma did not write. We do not know much about Kerma.

3rd Cataract

■ KERMA

4th Cataract

NAPATA ■

5th Cataract

NUBIA

■ MEROE

▲ Kerma was a city in Nubia.

Egypt was north of Kerma. Egypt had great armies. The armies conquered the city of Kerma. The armies burned Kerma.

▲ **Armies from Egypt conquered Kerma.**

What Was the Kingdom of Kush?

A new kingdom began in Nubia. The kingdom was the kingdom of Kush. The kingdom of Kush had a capital city. The city was **Napata**.

▲ A palace was built at Napata. The palace was in a mountain.

DID YOU KNOW?

The cities of Kush had many walls. This modern city in Sudan has many walls.

People from Napata went to Egypt. The people learned about Egyptian gods. The people learned about pyramids. The people learned about writing.

▲ People learned about Egyptian writing.

▲ People learned about Egyptian gods.

▲ People learned about Egyptian pyramids.

Egypt ruled the kingdom of Kush. Kush wanted to be free from Egypt. The Kush army conquered Egypt.

▲ Soldiers from Kush conquered Egypt.

PEOPLE TO KNOW

Piankhi was a king of Kush. Piankhi and his army conquered Egypt.

People from Kush ruled Egypt. The people ruled for eighty-five years. Then other people conquered Egypt. The Kush people left Egypt.

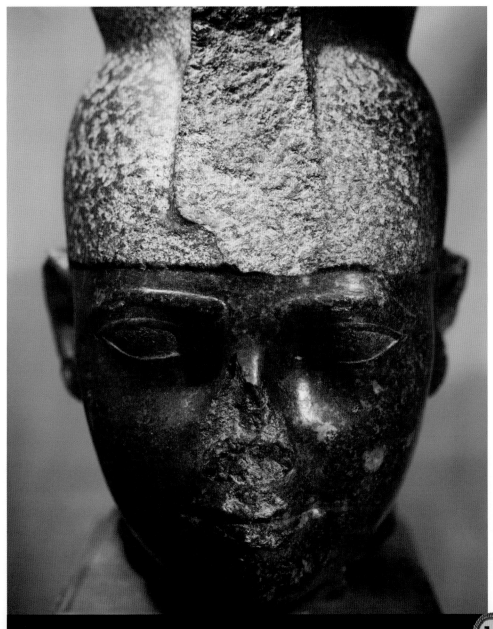

▲ **People from Kush ruled Egypt.**

What Was Meroe?

Meroe was a city. People moved to Meroe. Meroe was the capital of Kush.

▲ These pyramids were in Meroe.

Meroe had plenty of rain. Farmers grew crops. Forests were near Meroe. People used the trees for fires.

▲ Forests grew near Meroe.

People found iron near Meroe. Iron is a type of metal. People used iron to make tools and weapons.

▲ These iron tools were used with horses.

Meroe was an important city for hundreds of years. Then Meroe was not important. Maybe the land was not good for farming. Maybe people cut down all the trees.

▲ **These pyramids were in Meroe.**

Why Was the Kingdom of Kush Important?

Farmers of Kush grew many crops. Other people in Africa saw the crops. These people learned to grow the crops.

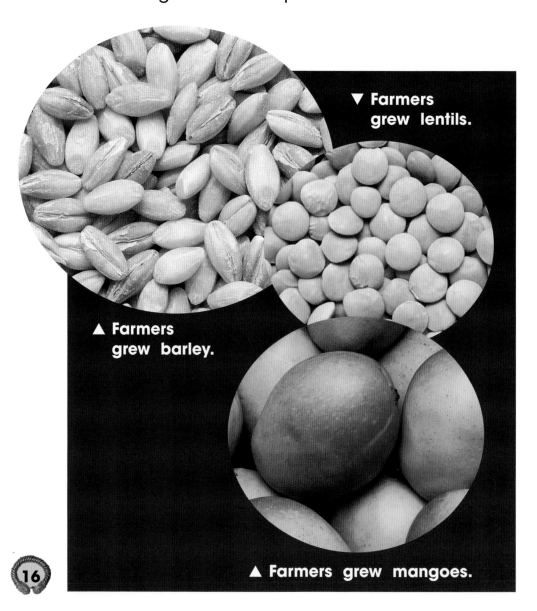

▼ Farmers grew lentils.

▲ Farmers grew barley.

▲ Farmers grew mangoes.

People of Kush made things from iron. The people made tools and weapons. The people made bowls and statues.

▲ People used iron to make things.
People still use iron to make things.

The people of Kush had gold. The people dug gold from the ground. They used gold to make beautiful things.

▲ Kush had gold.

The people of Kush made beautiful statues.

▲ This is a statue of Amun-Ra. This
statue guarded the king's palace.

IT'S A FACT

The people of Kush had
writing. Today, we cannot
read this writing. Maybe
we will learn to read the
writing. Then we will
know more about Kush.

19

Summary

Nubia was a region in Africa. Kush was a kingdom in Nubia. Meroe was an important city in the kingdom of Kush.

HISTORY OF KUSH

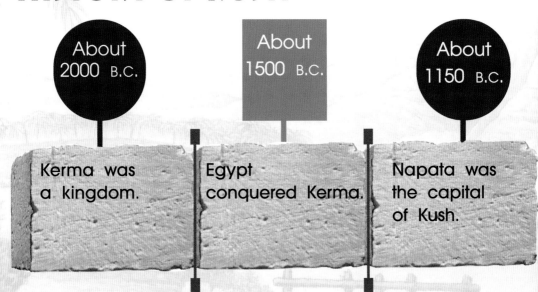

About 2000 B.C.

About 1500 B.C.

About 1150 B.C.

Kerma was a kingdom.

Egypt conquered Kerma.

Napata was the capital of Kush.

SOLVE THIS

Kerma was a kingdom in 2000 B.C. Other people conquered Meroe in 350 A.D. How many years were between these two times?

20

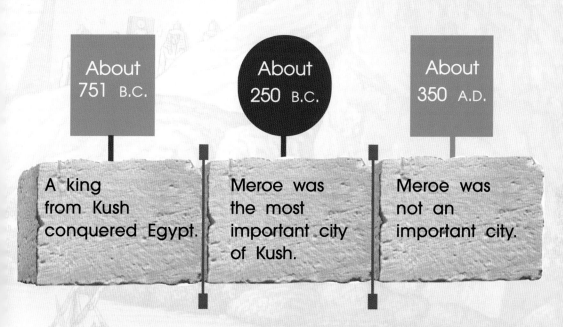

About 751 B.C.	About 250 B.C.	About 350 A.D.
A king from Kush conquered Egypt.	Meroe was the most important city of Kush.	Meroe was not an important city.

Think About It
1. What was Nubia?
2. Why did people live beside the Nile River?
3. Why was the kingdom of Kush important?

Glossary

Egypt a civilization north of Nubia

Egypt was beside the Nile River.

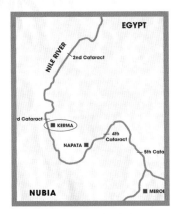

Kerma a capital city of Kush

Kerma was an important city.

kingdom people and lands ruled by a king

*Meroe was a **kingdom** in Nubia.*

Kush a kingdom in Nubia

*The kingdom of **Kush** was in Africa.*

Meroe an important city of the kingdom of Kush

*People found iron near **Meroe**.*

Napata a capital city of Kush

Napata was an important city of Kush.

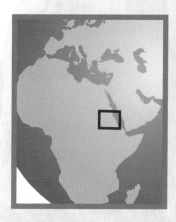

Nile River a long river in Africa

*The **Nile River** was in Egypt and Nubia.*

Nubia a region in Africa

*The kingdom of Kush was in **Nubia**.*

region a large area of land

*Nubia was a **region** in Africa.*

Index

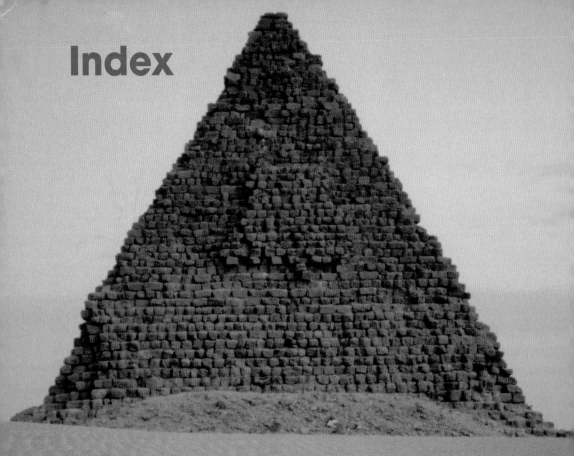